Math Practice for Principles of Microeconomics

Math Practice for Principles of Microeconomics

Carl Sutton Mapleton

Published by Econ Books Now
2017

First Printing: 2017

ISBN 978-1-387-15855-3

Published by: Econ Books Now

Ordering Information:

Special discounts may be available on quantity purchases by corporations, associations, educators, and others. For details, contact the publisher at the below listed email address.

econbooksnow@gmail.com

Contents

Introduction

Many students are required to take an introductory course in microeconomics in college, even if they have no plans to become economics majors.

Math is certainly a necessary tool used in all levels of economics, and it often helps to reinforce in a numerical way the concepts learned while studying economics.

Students often have varying levels of comfort with the mathematics which is used in economics. This can present challenges to both students and educators alike. An educator doesn't want advanced students getting bored by spending too much time on math, and doesn't want other students getting left behind by speeding through all the math practice. Students just want to get the best experience they can from the course.

This book is aimed to help both students and educators as a collection of the more math-intensive practice problems that are often seen in introductory microeconomics. There are no definition or concept questions – just collections of problems in which math is required. Students can use this for extra practice, and faculty can assign the book for students as needed.

The text is presented in workbook format. Students can show work, complete the problems, and check answers that are provided in the back of the text.

Further, the equations and problems are presented in a variety of ways to benefit students receiving different methods of instruction.

Problem Set A – Absolute and Comparative Advantage

A1. George and Abraham can each make pies or cakes. The table below shows how long it takes each of them to make each good.

	Time needed to make a pie	Time needed to make a cake
George	5 hours	2 hours
Abraham	6 hours	4 hours

a. Who has the absolute advantage in pie production?

b. Who has the absolute advantage in cake production?

c. Fill out the table below, showing the opportunity cost of each person making each good.

	Opportunity cost of making a pie	Opportunity cost of making a cake
George		
Abraham		

d. Who has the comparative advantage in producing pies?

e. Who has the comparative advantage in producing cakes?

A2. Here is a problem presented in a slightly different format. Instead of showing how long it takes to make goods, we are given information about how many goods can be made per time period.

Hint: This means the division in your math will have to be done in the other direction.

Mike and Jeff can each make steaks or pizzas.

	Steaks	Pizzas
Mike	Can make 8 per hour	Can make 4 per hour
Jeff	Can make 12 per hour	Can make 3 per hour

a. Who has the absolute advantage in steak production?

b. Who has the absolute advantage in pizza production?

c. Fill out the table below, showing the opportunity cost of each person making each good.

	Opportunity cost of making a steak	Opportunity cost of making a pizza
Mike		
Jeff		

A3. Sam and Joe can each make sandwiches or burgers. The table below shows how long it takes each of them to make each good.

	Time needed to make a burger	Time needed to make a sandwich
Sam	6 minutes	3 minutes
Joe	2 minutes	2 minutes

a. Fill out the table below, showing the opportunity cost of each person making each good.

	Opportunity cost of making a burger	Opportunity cost of making a sandwich
Sam		
Joe		

b. Who has the comparative advantage in producing burgers?

c. Who has the comparative advantage in producing sandwiches?

Assume that Sam and Joe each specialize in production according to their comparative advantage. Assume there is a 2 hour (120 minute) time period in which the two can produce food.

d. If Sam specializes in production according to his comparative advantage, what good does he produce during the time period? How many units of the good will he produce?

e. If Joe specializes in production according to his comparative advantage, what good does he produce during the time period? How many units of the good will he produce?

Bearing in mind the answers from parts (e) and (f), Sam and Joe each consider their opportunity costs of making burgers and sandwiches. Examining this, they determine a fair relative value in which a burger is worth 1.5 sandwiches.

In order to each have some of both goods, Sam and Joe trade. Joe gives 20 burgers to Sam, and Sam gives 30 sandwiches to Joe.

f. How many of each item does Joe have after the trade? Could Joe have produced this mixture of goods on his own in 120 minutes?

g. How many of each item does Sam have after the trade? Could Joe have produced this mixture of goods on his own in 120 minutes?

Problem Set B – Simple Supply and Demand

B1. Each of the following problems presents a demand and supply equation. Q_D is quantity demanded and Q_S is quantity supplied. Solve each system for the equilibrium price and quantity.

a. $Q_D = 86 - 4P$
     $Q_S = 9 + 7P$

b. $Q_D = 136 - P$
     $Q_S = 12 + 3P$

c. $Q_D = 384 - 4P$
     $Q_S = 8P$

d. $Q_D = 399 - 2P$
     $Q_S = -1 + 8P$

e. $Q_D = 449 - 5P$
     $Q_S = -2 + 6P$

f. $Q_D = 176 - 8P$
     $Q_S = 11 + 3P$

g. $Q_D = 228 - 8P$
     $Q_S = 12 + 4P$

h. $Q_D = 269 - 3P$
       $Q_S = 14P$

i. $Q_D = 247 - 8P$
       $Q_S = 9 + 6P$

j. $Q_D = 476 - 5P$
       $Q_S = 8 + 7P$

k. $Q_D = 650 - 8P$
       $Q_S = 6 + 6P$

l. $Q_D = 333 - 6P$
       $Q_S = 4 + P$

m. $Q_D = 390 - 4P$
       $Q_S = -2 + 4P$

n. $Q_D = 75 - 6P$
       $Q_S = 11 + 2P$

o. $Q_D = 202 - 5P$
       $Q_S = -1 + 2P$

Problem Set C – Advanced Supply and Demand

C1. Consider hamburgers as a good. You are given the following:

Demand: $Q_D = 700 - 10P + 10P_S$

Supply: $Q_S = -100 + 30P - 20C$

Where:

Q_D = quantity demanded

Q_S = quantity supplied

P = the price of hamburgers

P_S = the price of steak (a <u>substitute</u> good for hamburgers)

C = the marginal cost of producing hamburgers

a. Solve for equilibrium P* and Q* of hamburgers. Note that P* and Q* will be in terms of P_S and C.

b. Comparative statics problem: If the price of steak increases by 4 dollars, how will the equilibrium price and quantity of hamburgers change?

c. Comparative statics problem: If the marginal cost of hamburger production increases by 2 dollars, how will the equilibrium price and quantity of hamburgers change?

C2. Consider hamburgers as a good. You are given the following:

Demand: $Q_D = 900 - 15P + 20P_S - 12P_C + 5Y$
Supply: $Q_S = 30P - 10C$

Where:

Q_D = quantity demanded
Q_S = quantity supplied
P = the price of the good
P_S = the price of sandwiches (a <u>substitute</u> good)
P_F = the price of fries (a <u>complement</u> good)
Y = consumers income
C = the marginal cost of producing hamburgers

a. Solve for P* and Q*. Note that $P = P(P_S, P_F, Y, C)$ and $Q = Q(P_S, P_F, Y, C)$.

b. Suppose that P_S increases by \$3, P_F increases by \$1, Y increases by \$20, and C decreases by \$4. What will happen the equilibrium price and quantity?

c. Suppose that P_S decreases by \$9, P_F increases by \$12, Y increases by \$30, and C decreases by \$3. What will happen the equilibrium price and quantity?

C3. Consider the following market.

Demand: $Q_D = 200 - 5P$
Supply: $Q_S = -100 + 20P$

a. Find the price that will cause a shortage of 25 units in this market. Find the Q_D and Q_S at this price.

b. Find the price that will cause a surplus of 125 units in this market.

Problem Set D – Price Elasticity of Demand

For the following demand equations, use the point elasticity of demand formula to answer each of the questions.

Remember that the formula for point elasticity of demand is:

$$E = \frac{dQ}{dP} \times \frac{P}{Q}$$

D1. Consider the demand function $Q_D = 120 - 2P$.

a. Find the price elasticity of demand at P = $40. Also find the total revenue earned by the firm if it sells at this price.

b. Find the price elasticity of demand P = $20. Also find the total revenue earned by the firm if it sells at this price.

c. What is the unit elastic price? Find the total revenue earned by the firm if it sells at this price.

D2. Consider the demand function $Q_D = 150 - 3P$.

a. Find the price elasticity of demand at P = $10. Also find the total revenue earned by the firm if it sells at this price.

b. Find the price elasticity of demand at P = $30. Also find the total revenue earned by the firm if it sells at this price.

c. What is the unit elastic price? Find the total revenue earned by the firm if it sells at this price.

D3. Consider the demand function $Q_D = 250 - P$.

a. Find the price elasticity of demand at $P = \$50$. Also find the total revenue earned by the firm if it sells at this price.

b. Find the price elasticity of demand at $P = \$100$. Also find the total revenue earned by the firm if it sells at this price.

c. What is the unit elastic price? Find the total revenue earned by the firm if it sells at this price.

D4. Suppose the demand for all-day parking at campus is given by

$$Q_D = 20{,}000 - 800P$$

a. If the price for parking is $8, how much total revenue is collected?

b. What is the price elasticity of demand when the price is $8?

c. If the University Parking Office wants to increase their total revenue, should they increase or decrease the price from $8?

d. What price should the Parking Office set if they want to maximize their revenue?

Problem Set E – Rents and Profits

E1. The table below shows weekly figures for a bowling alley in town. The figures include explicit costs, implicit costs, and revenues.

Detail	Amount ($)
Subscription to TV package	600
Salaries Paid to Workers	12,500
Opportunity cost of owner's time	10,000
Electricity Bill	690
Opportunity cost of owned capital	5,500
Cost of Cleaning Supplies	4,400
Revenues	60,000

a. What is the total weekly accounting cost for this firm?

b. What is the total weekly accounting profit for this firm?

c. What is the weekly economic profit for this firm?

E2. The table below shows weekly figures for a restaurant in town. The figures include explicit costs, implicit costs, and revenues.

Detail	Amount ($)
Salaries Paid to Workers	8,100
Food Ingredient Costs	5,700
Insurance Payment on Equipment	690
Opportunity Cost of Owner's Time	9,000
Interest Paid on Line of Credit	1,250
Gas Bill	600
Revenues	21,000

a. What is the total weekly accounting cost for this firm?

b. What is the total weekly accounting profit for this firm?

c. What is the weekly economic profit for this firm?

Problem Set F – Simple Cost Equations

Recall the cost functions of firm production:

$$TC = TVC + TFC$$
$$ATC = AVC + AFC$$

$$ATC = \frac{TC}{Q}$$

$$AVC = \frac{TVC}{Q}$$

$$AFC = \frac{TFC}{Q}$$

$$MC = \frac{\Delta TC}{\Delta Q}$$

TC = total cost
TVC = total variable cost
TFC = total fixed cost
ATC = average total cost
AVC = average variable cost
AFC = average fixed cost
MC = marginal cost

Complete the tables on the next pages using the cost equations.

Q	TFC	TVC	TC	AFC	AVC	ATC	MC
0	120	0	120	--	--	--	--
1		1	121	120	1	121	1
2		6					
3			147				21
4						49	49
5		165					89
6					51		
7		511			73		
8			912				
9		1161					
10	120	1630	1750		163		

F2

Q	TFC	TVC	TC	AFC	AVC	ATC	MC
0	60	0	60	--	--	--	--
1	60	14	74	60	14	74	14
2	60	20	80	30	10	40	6
3		24					
4			92				
5					10		
6						24	
7							56
8							84
9		342	402				
10					50	56	158

Q	TFC	TVC	TC	AFC	AVC	ATC	MC
0				--	--	--	--
1		57					
2			152				
3		171					
4						70	
5					65		
6							107
7			607				
8		736		5			
9					105		
10					120		

Problem Set G – Productivity and Costs

Consider the following tables, where:

- L is the number of labor inputs
- TP is the total product of output (quantity produced) by the firm
- APL is the average product of labor
- MPL is the marginal product of labor
- MC is the marginal cost of output
- TFC is total fixed costs of production
- TVC is total variable costs of production
- TC is total costs of production
- AVC is average variable costs of production

G1. Fill out the following table, assuming each worker is paid a wage rate of w = $50. There are no fixed costs for the firm.

L	TP	APL	MPL	MC	TC	ATC
0	0	--	--	--		--
1	4					
2	12					
3	24					
4	40					
5	60					
6	75					
7	84					
8	86					

G2. a. Fill out the following table, assuming each worker is paid a wage rate of w = $60. Assume the firm has fixed costs of $10. Also, assume that labor is the only variable cost for the firm

L	TP	APL	MPL	MC	TFC	TVC	TC	AVC
0	0	--	--	--				--
1	10							
2	30							
3	60							
4	100							
5	135							
6	160							
7	175							
8	180							

b. If the price of this firm's output is $3 per unit, how many workers would it hire?

c. If the price of this firm's output is $6 per unit, how many workers would it hire?

d. If fixed costs increase from $10 to $30, how does your answer to the previous question change?

G3. a. Fill out the following table, assuming each worker is paid a wage rate of w = $100. Assume the firm has fixed costs of $20. Also, assume that labor is the only variable cost for the firm

L	TP	APL	MPL	MC	TFC	TVC	TC	AVC
0	0	--	--	--	20	0	20	--
1	12	12	12	8.33	20	100	120	8.33
2	27	13.5	15	6.67	20	200	220	7.41
3	45	15	18	5.56	20	300	320	6.67
4	61	15.25	16	6.25	20	400	420	6.56
5	75	15	14	7.14	20	500	520	6.67
6	87	14.5	12	8.33	20	600	620	6.90
7	96	13.71	9	11.11	20	700	720	7.29
8	102	12.75	6	16.67	20	800	820	7.84

b. If the price of this firm's output is $15 per unit, how many workers would it hire?

c. If the price of this firm's output is $10 per unit, how many workers would it hire?

Problem Set H – Output, Costs, and Profits in Perfectly Competitive Markets

H1. Suppose a competitive firm has a TC function of $TC = q^3 - 4q^2 + 10q + 10$. Therefore, $MC = 3q^2 - 8q + 10$.

Find each of the following:

a. The ATC function

b. The VC function

c. Fixed costs

d. The AVC function

e. The AFC function

f. The shutdown price for this firm

H2. Suppose a competitive firm has fixed costs in the short run of FC = 160. Its variable costs are given by TVC = 10q². The firm's marginal cost is MC = 20q. What is the break-even price for the firm?

H3. Consider a perfectly competitive market. The current market price is P = $42.

Suppose an individual firm in this industry has the following cost functions:

$$TC = q^2 + 315$$

$$ATC = q + \frac{315}{q}$$

$$MC = 2q$$

a. What quantity will be produced by this firm?

b. What is the profit or loss earned by this firm?

H4. Suppose that an individual firm in a perfectly competitive industry has the following:
$$TC = 0.4q^3 - 0.05q^2 + 3q + 10$$

$$ATC = 0.4q^2 - 0.05q + 3 + \frac{10}{q}$$

$$MC = 1.2q^2 - 0.1q + 3$$

Assume that the market price given to this firm is P = $33.

a. Find the quantity produced by this perfectly competitive firm. Round to the nearest whole quantity.

b. Using this rounded quantity of output, find the ATC per unit. Don't round the ATC value that you find.

c. Find the profits earned by the firm at this quantity of output.

H5. There are a total of X firms in a perfectly competitive market. Assume that each firm has the same costs, and will produce the same amount of output.

Each firm's cost function is $TC = 256 + q^2$, and any individual firm's marginal cost of production is given by $MC = 2q$. Note that q is the output level produced by an individual firm.

The market demand is by $P = 384 - 2Q$. Note that Q is the total industry output produced by all the firms. As a result, $Q = X*q$.

a. Assume the competitive market is long-run equilibrium. How much output will each firm produce?

b. What is the long-run equilibrium market price?

c. How many firms are in the market in this long run equilibrium?

Problem Set I – Market Efficiency and Gains from Trade

I1. Consider a competitive market where demand and supply are given by:

$$Q_D = 120 - 4P$$
$$Q_S = 2P$$

a. Find the equilibrium price and quantity

b. Find consumer surplus (CS) and producer surplus (PS) if the market is in equilibrium.

c. Suppose a price ceiling of $P = \$14$ is enforced on the market. Find the new quantity of goods that is traded at this price.

d. With this price ceiling, find the amount of CS and PS. Also, find the amount of deadweight loss (DWL) created by the price ceiling.

12. Consider a competitive market where demand and supply are given by:

$Q_D = 138 - 3P$
$Q_S = -2 + 2P$

a. Find the equilibrium price and quantity

b. Find consumer surplus (CS) and producer surplus (PS) if the market is in equilibrium.

c. Suppose a price ceiling of $P = \$16$ is enforced on the market. Find the new quantity of goods that is traded at this price.

d. With this price ceiling, find the amount of CS and PS. Also, find the amount of deadweight loss (DWL) created by the price ceiling.

13. Consider a competitive market where demand and supply are given by:

$$Q_D = 70 - 2P$$
$$Q_S = -10 + 2P$$

a. Find the equilibrium price and quantity

b. Find consumer surplus (CS) and producer surplus (PS) if the market is in equilibrium.

c. Suppose a price floor of P = $25 is enforced on the market. Find the new quantity of goods that is traded at this price.

d. With this price floor, find the amount of CS and PS. Also, find the amount of deadweight loss (DWL) created by the price floor.

Problem Set J – Monopoly

J1. A monopolist faces the following demand curve:

$$P = 560 - 10Q.$$

The firm has a constant marginal cost of MC = 20. There are no fixed costs. Since there are no fixed costs and MC is constant, MC = ATC.

a. What the marginal revenue (MR) function for the monopolist?

b. What is the monopolist's profit maximizing level of output?

c. What price will the profit maximizing monopolist charge?

d. How much profit will the monopolist make?

e. What is the value of consumer surplus generated in the market?

f. What is the deadweight loss resulting from the monopoly (compared to a market that would have produced where P = MC)?

J2. A natural monopoly faces the following demand curve:

$P = 1230 - 15Q.$

Cost functions for the firm are:

$$MC = 30$$

$$ATC = 30 + \frac{160}{q}$$

a. What is the monopolist's profit maximizing level of output?

b. What price will the profit maximizing monopolist charge?

c. How much profit will the monopolist make?

Problem Set K – Price Discrimination

K1. Suppose that Couchtown, a monopoly furniture store, is trying to get rid of an excess amount of inventory. The store has the following potential customers, and Couchtown knows their maximum willingness to pay for a couch. Each consumer is willing to buy one couch at the price listed. The table of consumers is below.

Consumer	Maximum Willingness To Pay ($)
Arnold	2,200
Bertha	2,000
Cammie	1,700
Daryl	1,500
Elijah	1,000
Franklin	800

a. Suppose the store sells couches at a single price to everyone. If the price is $900 per couch, who many couches will be sold? How much revenue will be received by Couchtown?

b. What single price will maximize revenue received by the firm?

c. If Couchtown could perfectly price discriminate, what is the highest possible revenue it could receive?

K2. In a monopolized market, there are two types of consumers in the market: Teens and Adults. The demands for the product for each type of consumers are:

Teens: $Q = 60 - 3P$ Adults: $Q = 60 - 2P$

There are no fixed costs. The marginal cost of production is constant at $MC = 10$.

a. Complete the table below. The table shows the separate demand for teens and adults, as well as the costs that would be involved with producing those quantities.

P	Teens (Q = 60 – 3P)				Adults (Q = 60 – 2P)				Single Price Total Profits
	Q	TR	TC	Profit	Q	TR	TC	Profit	
13	21	273	210	63	34	442	340	102	165
14	18	252	180	72	32	448	320	128	200
15	15	225	150	75	30	450	300	150	225
16	12	192	120	72	28	448	280	168	240
17	9	153	90	63	26	442	260	182	245
18	6	108	60	48	24	432	240	192	240
19	3	57	30	27	22	418	220	198	225
20	0	0	0	0	20	400	200	200	200
21	0	0	0	0	18	378	180	198	198

b. If the monopoly can price discriminate, what price would it charge to teens and adults? What would the total profits be?

c. If the monopoly cannot price discriminate and must charge a single price to everyone, what price and quantity would result? What would the total profits be?

K3. In a monopolized market, there are two types of consumers in the market: Teens and Adults. The demands for the product for each type of consumers are:

Teens: $Q = 240 - 5P$
Adults: $Q = 240 - 3P$

For production, the marginal cost is constant at $MC = 0$. There are no fixed costs.

a. Suppose the monopoly can price discriminate. What price will be charged to teenagers? How many units will teenagers buy?

b. What price will be charged to adults? How many units will adults buy?

c. How much total profit will the monopolist earn?

d. Consider a situation where the firm <u>cannot</u> price discriminate and must charge the same price to teens and adults. What is the price, quantity, and profit earned by the firm?

Problem Set L – Basic Game Theory

L1. The following game is a two player simultaneous game. The players are Player A and Player B. The strategies for Player A are Up and Down. The strategies for Player B are Left and Right. The payoffs are shown in the table. In each cell in the matrix, the number of the left is Player A's payoff and the number on the right is Player B's payoff.

		Player B	
		Left	Right
Player A	Up	10, 40	30, 50
	Down	20, 10	75, 45

a. Does Player A have a dominant strategy?

b. Does Player B have a dominant strategy?

c. Is there a Nash Equilibrium in pure strategies?

L2. Consider the following game:

		Player B	
		Left	Right
Player A	Up	60, 40	50, 60
	Down	70, 30	20, 10

a. Does player A have a dominant strategy?

b. Does Player B have a dominant strategy?

c. Is there a Nash Equilibrium in pure strategies?

L3. Consider the following game:

		Player B	
		Left	Right
Player A	Up	5, 3	4, 4
	Down	7, 2	3, 3

a. Does player A have a dominant strategy?

b. Does Player B have a dominant strategy?

c. Is there a Nash Equilibrium in pure strategies?

L4. Examine the following sequential game represented in tree form. Using backwards induction, find the sequentially rational equilibrium.

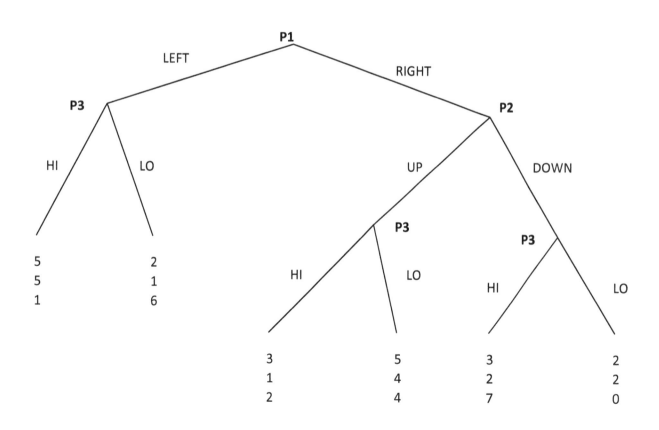

L5.

For each game below, find all dominant strategies by each player and any pure strategy Nash equilibria.

a.

		Player B		
		Paper	Rock	Scissors
Player A	Paper	0, 0	1, -1	-1, 1
	Rock	-1, 1	0, 0	1, -1
	Scissors	1, -1	-1, 1	0, 0

b.

		Zack		
		A	B	C
	A	0, 0	25, 40	5, 10
Yolanda	B	40, 25	0, 0	5, 15
	C	10, 5	15, 5	10, 10

c.

		Evander	
		Attack	Defend
	Punch	3, 5	2, 7
Mike	Kick	6, 6	1, 5
	Bite	1, 0	0, 0

Problem Set M – Taxes

M1. The market for jackets is given by:

Demand: $Q = 400 - 2P$
Supply: $Q = -80 + 4P$

a. Find the equilibrium price and quantity

Now, suppose a tax of $15 per jacket is imposed on the producers.

b. How much will consumers pay for jackets after the tax?

c. How much will producers receive per jacket after the tax?

d. What percentage of the tax will be paid by consumers?

e. What is the actual amount of tax dollars collected by the government? What is the DWL caused by the tax?

M2. The market for high-end gaming laptops is given by:

Demand: $Q = 6000 - 3P$
Supply: $Q = -100 + P$

a. Find the equilibrium price and quantity

Now, suppose a tax of $80 per laptop is imposed on the producers.

b. How much will consumers pay for laptops after the tax?

c. How much will producers receive per laptop after the tax?

d. What percentage of the tax will be paid by consumers?

e. What is the actual amount of tax dollars collected by the government? What is the DWL caused by the tax?

Problem Set N – Consumer Utility

N1. Complete the tables below.

Number of apples consumed	Total Utility	Marginal Utility
0	0	--
1	20	
2	35	
3	47	
4	57	
5	63	

Number of pears consumed	Total Utility	Marginal Utility
0	0	--
1		22
2		18
3		14
4		10
5		6

N2. Consider the table below. Bobby can buy one of three goods. The prices of three goods are given. Also, Bobby's marginal utilities of consumption are shown.

Good	Price	Marginal Utility
Jumbo Pizza Slice	$5	20
Burger	$3	18
Taco	$2	10

Which good will Bobby buy for lunch, assuming he can afford all three? Why?

N3. (Very advanced problem) Jonah has $300 to spend ($I = \$300$) on two goods: Ribs (R) and Chicken (C). Normally, the price of a rack of ribs is $P_R = \$12$, and the price of a whole chicken is $P_C = \$20$. Jonah enjoys ribs and chicken, but thinks the prices are too high, so he wants to use a discount.

Jonah has a choice of 3 discounts to use. The restaurant will only allow him to use one discount. A discount will effectively change Jonah's budget constraint.

- The College discount decreases the price of Chicken to $P_C = \$15$.
  Ribs are still $P_R = \$12$.
- The ECON discount decreases the price of Ribs to $P_R = \$8$.
  Chicken is still $P_C = \$20$.
- The Frequent Diner discount decreases both prices to $P_R = \$10$ and $P_C = \$18$.

a. Write down the 4 budget constraints (no discount, College, ECON, and Frequent Diner). The budget constraints should contain just two variables, P_R and P_C.
Hint: $I = C \times P_C + R \times P_R$

Assume Jonah's utility function for Ribs and Steak is
$$U = R^2 C^3$$
This means that marginal utilities are:
$$MU_R = 2RC^3$$
$$MU_C = 3R^2 C^2$$

b. Given the utility functions, income, and prices, what discount will Jonah choose?

Hint: There is a general procedure you can follow. For each discount, you must:
- Set the marginal rate of substitution equal to the price ratio to get the optimal consumption condition
- Use the optimal consumption and plug R or C into the budget constraint
- Get numerical values for R and C (how many of each Jonah will consume)
- Get a numerical utility value for the consumption
- Compare all 3 utilities to find the highest one, indicating the best discount for Jonah.

Solutions

A1

a. George
b. George

c.

	Opportunity cost of making a pie	Opportunity cost of making a cake
George	2.5 cakes	0.40 pies
Abraham	1.5 cakes	0.666 es

d. Abraham (he gives up the fewest cakes when making pie)
e. George (he gives up the fewest pies when making cake)

A2

a. Jeff
b. Mike

c.

	Opportunity cost of making a steak	Opportunity cost of making a pizza
Mike	0.5 pizzas	2 steaks
Jeff	0.25 pizzas	4 steaks

A3

a.

	Opportunity cost of making a burger	Opportunity cost of making a sandwich
Sam	2 sandwiches	0.5 burgers
Joe	1 sandwich	1 burger

b. Joe

c. Sam

d. 40 sandwiches

e. 60 burgers

f. Joe would have 40 burgers and 30 sandwiches. He could not have produced this mixture of goods on his own – it would have taken him 140 minutes.

g. Sam would have 20 burgers and 10 sandwiches. He could not have produced this mixture of goods on his own – it would have taken him 150 minutes to do so.

B1

a. $P^* = 7$ $Q^* = 58$

b. $P^* = 31$ $Q^* = 105$

c. $P^* = 32$ $Q^* = 256$

d. $P^* = 40$ $Q^* = 319$

e. $P^* = 41$ $Q^* = 244$

f. $P^* = 15$ $Q^* = 56$

g. $P^* = 18$ $Q^* = 84$

h. $P^* = 37$ $Q^* = 158$

i. $P^* = 17$ $Q^* = 111$

j. $P^* = 39$ $Q^* = 281$

k. $P^* = 46$ $Q^* = 282$

l. $P^* = 47$ $Q^* = 51$

m. $P^* = 49$ $Q^* = 194$

n. $P^* = 8$ $Q^* = 27$

o. $P^* = 29$ $Q^* = 57$

C1

a. $P^* = 20 + 0.25P_S + 0.5C$ $Q^* = 500 + 7.5P_S - 5C$

b. First, note the coefficients on P_S in our P* and Q* that we found.

In P*, the coefficient on P_S is 0.25, which means that for every dollar increase in P_S, we expect P* to increase by 0.25 dollars. Thus, if P_S increases by $4, P* (hamburger price) increases by $1.

In Q*, the coefficient on P_S is 7.5. This means that for every dollar increase in P_S, we expect Q* to increase by 7.5 units. Thus, if P_S increases by $4, Q* (hamburger quantity) increases by 30.

c. Following the same logic as in part (b), we can examine the coefficient on C in our P* and Q*. If C increases by $2, it follows that P* will increase by $1, and Q* will decrease by 10 units.

C2

a. $P^* = 20 + \frac{4}{9}P_S - \frac{4}{15}P_F + \frac{1}{9}Y + \frac{2}{9}C$ $Q^* = 600 + \frac{40}{9}P_S - 8P_F + \frac{10}{3}Y - \frac{10}{3}C$

b. P* will increase by $2.4.   Q* will increase by 85.33.

c. P* will decrease by $4.53,   Q* will decrease by 26

C3

a. Set up the solution creating by shortage of 100 units. $Q_D = Q_S + 100$
Solving yields P = $10
$Q_D = 600 - 10(10) \rightarrow$ $Q_D = 500$
$Q_S = 40(10) \rightarrow$ $Q_S = 400$
At a price of P = $10, we have a shortage of 100 units.

b. P = $13.5, $Q_D = 465$, $Q_S = 540$

D1
a. $E_D = -2$ TR = $1,600
b. $E_D = -0.5$ TR = $1,600
c. P = $30   TR = $1,800

D2
a. $E_D = -0.25$ TR = $1,200
b. $E_D = -1.5$ TR = $1,800
c. P = $25   TR = $1,875

D3
a. $E_D = -0.25$ TR = $10,000
b. $E_D = -0.666$ TR = $15,000
c. P = $125   TR = $15,625

D4

a. TR = $108,800 (you must first find that Q = 13,600 at the given price)

b. $E_D = -0.4706$

c. The demand is inelastic at the price of $8. Thus, the parking officials should raise the price for parking.

d. The midpoint price (where demand is unit elastic) is P = $12.5. This price will generate the maximum revenue of TR = $125,000.

E1
a. $18,190
b. $41,810
c. $26,310

E2
a. $16,340
b. $4,660
c. –$4,340 (A negative economic profit is also called losses. It means the firm is doing worse than its opportunity cost).

F1

Q	TFC	TVC	TC	AFC	AVC	ATC	MC
0	120	0	120	--	--	--	--
1	120	1	121	120	1	121	1
2	120	6	126	60	3	63	5
3	120	27	147	40	9	49	21
4	120	76	196	30	19	49	49
5	120	165	285	24	33	57	89
6	120	306	426	20	51	71	141
7	120	511	631	17.14	73	90.14	205
8	120	792	912	15	99	114	281
9	120	1161	1281	13.33	129	142.3	369
10	120	1630	1750	12	163	175	469

F2

Q	TFC	TVC	TC	AFC	AVC	ATC	MC
0	60	0	60	--	--	--	--
1	60	14	74	60	14	74	14
2	60	20	80	30	10	40	6
3	60	24	84	20	8	28	4
4	60	32	92	15	8	23	8
5	60	50	110	12	10	22	18
6	60	84	144	10	14	24	34
7	60	140	200	8.571	20	28.57	56
8	60	224	284	7.5	28	35.5	84
9	60	342	402	6.667	38	44.67	118
10	60	500	560	6	50	56	158

F3

Q	TFC	TVC	TC	AFC	AVC	ATC	MC
0	40	0	40	--	--	--	--
1	40	57	97	40	57	97	57
2	40	112	152	20	56	76	55
3	40	171	211	13.33	57	70.33	59
4	40	240	280	10	60	70	69
5	40	325	365	8	65	73	85
6	40	432	472	6.67	72	78.67	107
7	40	567	607	5.71	81	86.71	135
8	40	736	776	5	92	97	169
9	40	945	985	4.44	105	109.4	209
10	40	1200	1240	4	120	124	255

G1

L	TP	APL	MPL	MC	TC	ATC
0	0	--	--	--	0	--
1	4	4	4	25	50	12.5
2	12	6	8	12.5	100	8.33
3	24	8	12	8.33	150	6.25
4	40	10	16	6.25	200	5
5	60	12	20	5	250	4.17
6	75	12.5	15	6.67	300	4
7	84	12	9	11.1	350	4.17
8	86	10.8	2	50	400	4.65

G2

a.

L	TP	APL	MPL	MC	TFC	TVC	TC	AVC
0	0	--	--	--	10	0	10	--
1	10	10	10	6	10	60	70	6
2	30	15	20	3	10	120	130	4
3	60	20	30	2	10	180	190	3
4	100	25	40	1.5	10	240	250	2.4
5	135	27	35	1.71	10	300	310	2.22
6	160	26.7	25	2.4	10	360	370	2.25
7	175	25	15	4	10	420	430	2.4
8	180	22.5	5	12	10	480	490	2.67

b. Each worker has a wage rate of $60. Thus, we need to see if the cost of hiring the worker ($60) is greater than the value of the product they produce at the margin. This value is referred to as marginal revenue product (MRP) and is found by taking the price multiplied by the marginal product of the worker. With a price of $3, the workers would have to produce at least 20 units at the margin to be hired. Thus, the firm will hire 6 workers. It will not hire the seventh worker. Note that the first worker has MRP < 60, but we are experiencing increasing marginal product here, so the firm will hire the first worker and continue to hire more workers beyond this.

c. In this case, the firm would hire 7 workers, but would not hire the eighth worker.

d. The answer wouldn't change. Fixed costs do not play a role in the decision at the margin.

G3

a.

L	TP	APL	MPL	MC	TFC	TVC	TC	AVC
0	0	--	--	--	20	0	20	--
1	12	12	12	8.33	20	100	120	8.33
2	27	13.5	15	6.67	20	200	220	7.41
3	45	15	18	5.56	20	300	320	6.67
4	61	15.3	16	6.25	20	400	420	6.56
5	75	15	14	7.14	20	500	520	6.67
6	87	14.5	12	8.33	20	600	620	6.9
7	96	13.7	9	11.1	20	700	720	7.29
8	102	12.8	6	16.7	20	800	820	7.84

b. Recall that the wage rate is $w = \$100$.
At a price of $15, the firm would hire 7 workers.

c. At a price of $10 per unit, the firm would hire 6 workers.

H1

a. $ATC = \dfrac{q^3 - 4q^2 + 10q + 10}{q}$

b. $VC = q^3 - 4q^2 + 10q$

c. $FC = 10$

d. $AVC = \dfrac{q^3 - 4q^2 + 10q}{q} \rightarrow AVC = q^2 - 4q + 10$

e. $AFC = \dfrac{10}{q}$

f. The shutdown price occurs at the minimum of the AVC. This is where the MC intersects the AVC, so we can set AVC = MC to find this point.

$AVC = q^2 - 4q + 10 = 3q^2 - 8q + 10 = MC$

Solving this yields q = 2. At q = 2, MC = AVC = 6.
Thus, the shutdown price is P = \$6. In other words, if the price falls below P = \$6, the firm will shut down in the short run and produce q = 0.

H2

The break-even price for a firm is the minimum of Average Total Cost.
This occurs where MC = ATC. Average Total Cost is TC/q where q is the quantity of output.
Total Cost = TFC + TVC, so average total cost ATC equals
$\dfrac{160 + 10q^2}{q}$. Setting this equal to 20q and solving for q, q = 4.
When q = 4, MC = 80.
Therefore, at q = 5, MC = ATC = 80. Thus, the minimum of the ATC is 80. This is the break-even price. If the price is above 80, the firm will make a profit. If the price is less than 80, the firm will experience a loss.

H3

a. Quantity can be solved by setting P = MC. We get q = 21.

b. There are two ways to find profit. The first is to take total revenue subtract total cost. The second is to take quantity multiplied by average profit per unit.

First method
TR = 42 * 21 = 882
TC is found by evaluating the TC function at q = 21
TC = 756
Thus, profit = 882 − 756 = $126

Second method
Average profit is P − ATC. At 21 units, ATC = 36, so average profit is $6 per unit. Multiply this by 21 units to get profit = $126.

H4

a. Set P = MC

$$33 = 1.2q^2 - 0.1q + 3$$

Put it in a form that we can solve using the quadratic equation

$$0 = 1.2q^2 - 0.1q - 30$$

Solving yields q = 5.042. Round this to q = 5.

b. Plug in q = 5 into the ATC function

$$ATC = 0.4(5)^2 - 0.05(5) + 3 + \frac{10}{(5)}$$

This gives a result of ATC = $14.75

c. Use ATC = $14.75 and a price of P = $33, the average profit per unit is $18.25. Multiply this by the quantity of 5 to get total profit = $91.25.

H5

a. At long run equilibrium, we know that price will be equal to the break-even price, which is the minimum of the ATC. We know that the MC curve passes through the minimum of the ATC. Use this to find the output level q where ATC is minimized for each firm.

$$TC = 256 + q^2 \quad \rightarrow \quad ATC = \frac{256 + q^2}{q}$$

Set ATC = MC to find solve for the q at the minimum ATC.

$$ATC = MC \quad \rightarrow \quad \frac{256 + q^2}{q} = 2q \quad \rightarrow \quad q = 16$$

Thus, each firm is producing q = 16 units of output.

b. In perfect competition, we know that P = MC = MR for each individual firm. We know that all firms face the same price as well.
Set P = MC to find the price.

$$P = MC \rightarrow P = 2q \rightarrow P = 2(16) \rightarrow P = 32$$

The market price is P = $32.

c. We must use the market demand function and solve for X. Use

$$P = 384 - 2Q$$

And sub in for P, and remember that Q = X*q. Also, recall that q = 16.

$$32 = 384 - 32X \quad \rightarrow \quad X = 11$$

Thus, in this competitive market, the market price is $32, and there are 11 firms producing 16 units each.

I1

a. P* = 20, Q* = 40

b. CS = $200, PS = $400

c. Q = 28 (with the price ceiling, the new quantity will be determined by the sellers wanting to sell fewer units a lower price)

d. CS = $350, PS = $196, DWL = $54

I2

a. P* = 28, Q* = 54

b. CS = $486, PS = $729

c. Q = 30

d. CS = $750, PS = $225, DWL = $240

I3

a. P* = 20, Q* = 30

b. CS = $225, PS = $225

c. Q = 20 (with the price floor, the new quantity will be determined by the buyers wanting to buy fewer units a higher price)

d. CS = $100, PS = $300, DWL = $50

J1

a. MR = 560 – 20Q

b. Q = 27

c. P = 290

d. Profit = 7,290

e. This is the area below the demand curve and above the price up to the number of units purchased. Drawing a graph may help with the area of the triangle.
CS = 3,645

f. This is the triangle under the demand curve and above the MC function to the right of the quantity purchased. The competitive quantity is Q = 54.
DWL = 3,645

Note that in this case, CS happens to equal DWL. You can also see that the competitive quantity is twice that of the monopoly quantity. This is not always the case, but only occurs in the simple example where MC is constant and demand is linear.

J2

a. Q = 40

b. P = 330

c. Profit = 11,840

K1

a. Everyone except Franklin would buy a couch. The total revenue would be $4,500 (5 couches at $900 each)

b. Selling at $1,500 would yield a revenue of $6,000. The top four consumers would buy a couch.

c. With perfect price discrimination, Couchtown could just charge each person their maximum willingness to pay, and get a total of $9,200 in revenues.

K2

a.

P	Teens ($Q = 60 - 3P$)				Adults ($Q = 60 - 2P$)				Single Price Total Profits
	Q	TR	TC	Profit	Q	TR	TC	Profit	
13	21	273	210	63	34	442	340	102	165
14	18	252	180	72	32	448	320	128	200
15	15	225	150	75	30	450	300	150	225
16	12	192	120	72	28	448	280	168	240
17	9	153	90	63	26	442	260	182	245
18	6	108	60	48	24	432	240	192	240
19	3	57	30	27	22	418	220	198	225
20	0	0	0	0	20	400	200	200	200
21	0	0	0	0	18	378	180	198	198

b. Teens would get a price of $15 and buy 15 units.
Adults would get a price of $20 and buy 20 units.
The profit from teens would be $75, and the profit from adults would be $200.
Thus, the total profit would be $275.

c. The single price would be P = $17. 35 units would be sold (9 to teens and 26 to adults). The profit is $245.

K3

a. Teen price = $24, Teen quantity = 120
b. Adult price = $40, Adult quantity = 120
c. Total profit is $7680 ($2,880 from teens and $4,800 from adults)

L1

a. Down

b. Right

c. The pure strategy Nash Equilibrium is "Down" and "Right".

L2

a. No

b. No

c. There are two pure strategy Nash Equilibria. Up/Right and Down/Left.

L3

a. No

b. Right

c. The pure strategy Nash Equilibrium is "Up" and "Right".

L4

We will reach the payoff (3, 3, 4). The strategies for Players 1, 2, and 3 will be (Right, Up, Lo).

L5

a. There are no dominant strategies and no pure strategy Nash Equilibria.

b. There are no dominant strategies. There are three pure strategy Nash Equilibria: (Yolanda B, Zack A); (Yolanda A, Zack B); (Yolanda C, Zack C)

c. There are no dominant strategies. There are two pure strategy Nash Equilibria: (Kick, Attack); (Punch, Defend)
Interestingly, Mike has a <u>dominated</u> strategy. It is never in his best interest to Bite.

M1

a. $P* = 80$, $Q* = 240$

b. For a tax t = $15 imposed on the producers, the supply curve does a vertical shift of $15.
We can further picture this by taking 15 dollars away from each unit the firm sells.
Mathematically, we can do this supply shift by replacing the variable
P with (P − 15) and solve.

Set the "after tax" supply equal to demand and solve. This will get us a price.
$$-80 + 4(P - 15) = 400 - 2P$$
Solving yields P = 90.
We found a price of P = $90, but is this the price the seller receives (P_S) or the price the
buyer pays (P_B)? It is Pb, since it is on the demand curve. (we used the "after tax" supply
curve). Thus, P_B = $90. This is the price the buyer pays.

c. To find out how much producers receive, all we need to do is subtract the tax amount
from what the consumers pay. The sellers receive $75.

d. Consumers originally paid $80, and now pay $90, which is a $10 increase. Thus,
consumers pay $10 of the $15 tax, or 2/3 of the tax. Producers pay the remaining $5, or 1/3
of the tax.

e. We need to first figure out the number of units traded after the tax. Using our demand
and supply equations, we can plug the price $90 into demand, or plug in $75 into supply to
get the after tax quantity.
The new quantity traded after the tax is Q = 220.
Total tax revenue received is 200 * 15 = $3,300
Deadweight loss is $150. This is the triangle formed by the height equal to the tax amount
and a width equal to the reduction in units traded.

M2

a. $P* = 1,525$, $Q* = 1,425$
b. Consumers will pay $1,545 after the tax
c. Sellers will receive $1,465 after the tax
d. The consumers pay 1/4 of the tax.
e. Total tax revenue generated is $109,200. The DWL created is $2,400.

N1

Number of apples consumed	Total Utility	Marginal Utility
0	0	--
1	20	20
2	35	15
3	47	12
4	57	10
5	63	6

Number of pears consumed	Total Utility	Marginal Utility
0	0	--
1	22	22
2	40	18
3	54	14
4	64	10
5	70	6

N2

Assuming Bobby will just buy one of the food items, he will purchase the burger. It gives him the highest marginal utility per dollar spent.

N3

a.

Use $I = C \times P_C + R \times P_R$ for each discount.

No discount:	$300 = 20C + 12R$
College:	$300 = 15C + 12R$
ECON:	$300 = 20C + 8R$
Frequent Diner:	$300 = 18C + 10R$

b.

If we imagine a graph where Ribs are on the vertical axis and Chicken is on the horizontal, we have the following:

$$MRS = \frac{MU_C}{MU_R}$$

and

$$Price\ Ratio = Slope\ of\ Budget\ Constraint = \frac{P_C}{P_R}$$

The MRS will be the same for each discount. Preferences don't change, only prices.

$$MRS = \frac{MU_C}{MU_R} = \frac{3R^2 C^2}{2RC^3}$$

$$\rightarrow MRS = \frac{3R}{2C}$$

We can use this MRS for all 3 discounts we test.

N3 (continued)

College discount

Note that for this discount, $P_C = \$15$. $P_R = \$12$
Set MRS = Price ratio for optimal consumption. We can solve for R in terms of C.
$$\frac{3R}{2C} = \frac{15}{12} \quad \rightarrow \quad R = \frac{5}{6}C$$

Plug this into the College budget constraint.
$$300 = 15C + 12R$$
$$300 = 15C + 12\left(\frac{5}{6}C\right)$$
Thus,
$$C = 12$$

How can we solve for R? We know that
$$R = \frac{5}{6}C$$
Thus,
$$R = 10$$

We can verify - are we spending all our money?

$$Ribs: \; P_R \times R = 12 \times 10 = 120 = \frac{2}{5} \times 300$$
$$Chicken: \; P_C \times C = 15 \times 12 = 180 = \frac{3}{5} \times 300$$

Verification can help us double check to make sure our answer is correct.

What is the total utility for the College discount?
$$U = R^2 C^3$$
$$U = 10^2 12^3$$

Thus,

$$U_{College} = 172,800$$

ECON discount

Note that for this discount, $P_C = \$20$. $P_R = \$8$
Set MRS = Price ratio for optimal consumption. We can solve for R in terms of C.

$$\frac{3R}{2C} = \frac{20}{8} \quad \rightarrow \quad R = \frac{5}{3}C$$

Plug this into the ECON budget constraint.

$$300 = 20C + 8R$$
$$300 = 20C + 8\left(\frac{5}{3}C\right)$$

Thus,

$$C = 9$$

How can we solve for R? We know that

$$R = \frac{5}{3}C$$

Thus,

$$R = 15$$

We can verify - are we spending all our money?

$$Ribs: P_R \times R = 8 \times 15 = 120 = \frac{2}{5} \times 300$$
$$Chicken: P_C \times C = 20 \times 9 = 180 = \frac{3}{5} \times 300$$

Verification can help us double check to make sure our answer is correct.

What is the total utility for the ECON discount?

$$U = R^2C^3$$
$$U = 15^2 9^3$$

Thus,

$$U_{ECON} = 164,025$$

N3 (continued)

Frequent Diner discount

Note that for this discount, $P_C = \$18.$ $P_R = \$10$
Set MRS = Price ratio for optimal consumption. We can solve for R in terms of C.

$$\frac{3R}{2C} = \frac{18}{10} \quad \rightarrow \quad R = \frac{6}{5}C$$

Plug this into the Frequent Diner budget constraint.

$$300 = 18C + 10R$$

$$300 = 18C + 10\left(\frac{6}{5}C\right)$$

Thus,

$$C = 10$$

How can we solve for R? We know that

$$R = \frac{6}{5}C$$

Thus,

$$R = 12$$

We can verify - are we spending all our money?

$$Ribs\text{: } P_R \times R = 10 \times 12 = 120 = \frac{2}{5} \times 300$$

$$Chicken\text{: } P_C \times C = 18 \times 10 = 180 = \frac{3}{5} \times 300$$

Verification can help us double check to make sure our answer is correct.

What is the total utility for the Frequent Diner discount?

$$U = R^2 C^3$$
$$U = 12^2 10^3$$

Thus,

$$U_{Frequent\ Diner} = 144,000$$

N3 (continued)

Overall, we have the following:

$$U_{College} = 172{,}800$$

$$U_{ECON} = 164{,}025$$

$$U_{Frequent\ Diner} = 144{,}000$$

Jonah will choose the College discount. It gives him the highest utility.